What's it like to be a...
GROCER

Written by Shelley Wilks
Illustrated by Marcy Dunn Ramsey

Troll Associates

| **Special Consultants:** Ronald and Diane Nahass, *Proprietors* *Fish, Fruits & Fancy Market, Waldwick, New Jersey.* |

Library of Congress Cataloging-in-Publication Data

Wilks, Shelley.
    What's it like to be a grocer / by Shelley Wilks; illustrated by
Marcy Dunn Ramsey.
        p.   cm.—(Young careers)
    Summary: Depicts what it is like to run a small grocery store,
describing such tasks as picking out fresh produce at the city
market, stocking the shelves, and making deliveries.
    ISBN 0-8167-1805-9 (lib. bdg.)   ISBN 0-8167-1806-7 (pbk.)
    1. Grocers—Juvenile literature.   2. Grocery trade—Juvenile
literature. [1. Grocery trade.   2. Occupations.]   I. Ramsey,
Marcy Dunn, ill.   II. Title.
HD8039.G8W54   1990
381´.148´02373—dc20   89-34394

What's it like to be a...
GROCER

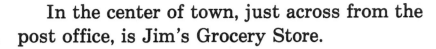

In the center of town, just across from the post office, is Jim's Grocery Store.

It's a pretty little store with blue and white
striped awnings and windows filled with all sorts
of good things to eat. Here comes Jim—he
owns the store. Jim is getting ready for another
busy day.

It is seven o'clock. Jim does not open his store until nine o'clock. But he has been hard at work since early this morning.

On Monday mornings, Jim gets up before
sunrise. He goes into the city. In the city is a
big fruit and vegetable market. Farmers from all
over the country ship their crops to market to be
sold.

Although most people in the city are still asleep, the market is a busy, busy place. Some people are unloading new shipments. Others are selling their produce from stands.

GRAPES

And still other people are going from stand
to stand, buying and ordering what they need.
Jim needs a variety of fresh fruits and
vegetables for his customers.

Carefully, he picks a box of oranges and
grapefruits from Florida. He buys potatoes from
Idaho; apples and pears from Washington;
broccoli and string beans from New York; and
tomatoes from New Jersey.

11

Then Jim notices fresh lettuce from California and cucumbers from Florida. He buys some and also buys boxes of lemons and limes.

On the loading dock, Jim puts his purchases into his truck, and off he goes.

Soon he is back at the store. The front of the store is where customers pick out the things they want to buy.

AM7340

13

In the back, Jim keeps an extra supply of everything he sells.

There is much to do before the store opens.
First, Jim arranges his fruits and vegetables in
the refrigerated case. The cool air will keep
everything fresh and tasty.

"Good morning, Jim!" calls Janie. Janie is Jim's helper. She helps Jim wait on customers and stock shelves.

A delivery arrives from a bakery. Janie checks the order of bread and other baked goods, while Jim opens the cash register.

Next a dairy truck arrives. Jim will have
fresh milk, eggs, and cheese for his customers.

And just before opening, a meat packer
arrives with a selection of sandwich meats for
Jim's deli counter.

At last everything is ready. Jim unlocks the
door and hangs up the OPEN sign. Janie makes
a display of fresh fruit in front of the store.

Just in time! Jim's first customer is here.
Mrs. Roberts is having friends to lunch. She
needs some fresh rolls.

"Jim," she says, "this fruit looks delicious."
She buys some oranges and grapefruits.

Jim's store is busy all morning. Carol and her mother and sister stop by for milk. They also buy some string beans for dinner and some lemons to make lemonade.

At lunch time, the postal workers and many
other people stop by for something to eat.
Behind his deli counter, Jim makes sandwiches.
He knows most of his customers by name and is
always glad to see them.

When the lunch crowd goes back to work, Jim leaves Janie in charge of the store. He must go out to make some deliveries, and then go to an important meeting.

First, he delivers some canned goods and fresh fruit to Mr. Olsen. Then he drops off some eggs, milk, butter, cheese, and bread at Mrs. Clark's house. Jim is always happy to deliver orders to his good customers.

After finishing his deliveries, Jim arrives at a large warehouse. A warehouse is a big building with lots of space in which to keep things. Jim is meeting with grocers from several nearby towns. They all store things in the warehouse.

By combining their orders, the grocers can buy in large quantities and save money. They keep their large orders in the warehouse. Bit by bit, the grocers move the warehouse items into their stores.

Jim and his friends each list what they want to order. They make one long list. This month, it's Alisa's turn to order everything and make sure everyone gets his or her share of the order. Next month, someone else will take a turn.

After the meeting, Jim goes to his section of the warehouse. It is filled with canned soups and vegetables, bottles of juice, pickles, ketchup, paper cups, towels, and tissues. Jim sees he needs more paper towels, tissues, and fruit juice. He adds them to his order.

Back at the store, Jim finds he has many customers. Some children saw the display of fruit outside the store. Jenny wants an apple. Paul wants a pear.

The door jingles again. It is Mr. Schmidt. He needs a few things for his supper. He sees the lettuce and cucumbers. Then he spots the tomatoes. Soon he has everything he needs for a fresh, delicious salad.

It has been a busy day. Jim locks the door
and counts the money.

Tomorrow, Jim will be in early again. He has to check his stock. He is expecting another delivery. And, of course, there will be lots and lots of customers passing through Jim's Grocery Store!